STEM IN THE WORLD CUP

BY MEG MARQUARDT

CONTENT CONSULTANT

JESSE WILCOX, PHD
ASSISTANT PROFESSOR OF STEM EDUCATION
SIMPSON COLLEGE

SportsZone

An Imprint of Abdo Publishing
abdobooks.com

ABDOBOOKS.COM

Published by Abdo Publishing, a division of ABDO, PO Box 398166, Minneapolis, Minnesota 55439. Copyright © 2020 by Abdo Consulting Group, Inc. International copyrights reserved in all countries. No part of this book may be reproduced in any form without written permission from the publisher. SportsZone™ is a trademark and logo of Abdo Publishing.

Printed in the United States of America, North Mankato, Minnesota
082019
012020

THIS BOOK CONTAINS RECYCLED MATERIALS

Cover Photo: Rich Graessle/Icon Sportswire/AP Images
Interior Photos: John Walton/URN:43882688/Press Association/AP Images, 4–5; Kunihiko Miura/The Yomiuri Shimbun/AP Images, 7; Kyodo/AP Images, 8; Shutterstock Images, 11, 24, 37 (bottom); Francisco Seco/AP Images, 12–13; Bob Thomas Sports Photography/Getty Images, 15; Martin Meissner/AP Images, 16; Red Line Editorial, 18, 44; Anke Waelischmiller/Sven Simon/picture-alliance/dpa/AP Images, 20–21; Alexander Zemlianichenko/AP Images, 23; Miguel Schincariol/AFP/Getty Images, 25; Elmar Kremser/SVEN SIMON/picture-alliance/dpa/AP Images, 26; Lou Avers/picture-alliance/dpa/AP Images, 28–29; Simon Holmes/NurPhoto/Getty Images, 31; Maddie Meyer - FIFA/FIFA/Getty Images, 32; Elise Amendola/AP Images, 34; CB2/ZOB/Supplied by WENN.com/Newscom, 36; Daniel Karmann/picture-alliance/dpa/AP Images, 37 (top); Beto Chagas/Shutterstock Images, 37 (middle); Pierre Stevenin/Zuma Wire/Cal Sport Media/AP Images, 38–39; Charlotte Wilson/Offside/Getty Images, 41; Matthias Schrader/AP Images, 42

Editor: Marie Pearson
Series Designer: Dan Peluso

LIBRARY OF CONGRESS CONTROL NUMBER: 2019941988

PUBLISHER'S CATALOGING-IN-PUBLICATION DATA
Names: Marquardt, Meg, author.
Title: STEM in the World Cup / by Meg Marquardt
Description: Minneapolis, Minnesota : Abdo Publishing, 2020 | Series: STEM in the greatest sports events | Includes online resources and index.
Identifiers: ISBN 9781532190582 (lib. bdg.) | ISBN 9781644943168 (pbk.) | ISBN 9781532176432 (ebook)
Subjects: LCSH: World Cup (Soccer)--Juvenile literature. | Sports sciences--Juvenile literature. | Applied science--Juvenile literature. | Soccer--Juvenile literature. | Physics--Juvenile literature.
Classification: DDC 796.015--dc23

TABLE OF CONTENTS

1 SCORING GOALS WITH STEM 4

2 SOCCER SCIENCE 12

3 GAME TECH 20

4 ENGINEERING THE GAMES 28

5 MATH AND NUMBERS 38

GLOSSARY 46
MORE INFORMATION 47
ONLINE RESOURCES 47
INDEX 48
ABOUT THE AUTHOR 48

Angles are one element of math that players use frequently in the World Cup.

CHAPTER 1

SCORING GOALS WITH STEM

The Women's World Cup game is on the line. A defender chases down a striker. The striker has the ball and is running toward the goal. The defender knows she has to stop the striker. But the striker is running too fast to catch before she shoots the ball.

The defender quickly studies the angles and looks at how fast the ball is traveling. She sprints until she is just behind the striker. Then she throws herself into a slide. She extends her leg. The slide has to be timed perfectly. One wrong move, and she will slide into the striker. A foul in the goal box would be disastrous.

But the defender has practiced this move a hundred times. She is one of the best. She slides, and her foot hits the ball. It rolls out of bounds. The scoring opportunity is stopped. The defender's team still has a chance to make it to the Women's World Cup final.

PLAYING ON THE BIGGEST STAGE

The World Cup is the world's biggest sporting event. The Fédération Internationale de Football Association (FIFA) runs the event. Men compete in the World Cup, and women compete in the Women's World Cup. Both tournaments showcase the world's top soccer players. Many of these players play on professional teams all over the world. In international tournaments such as the World Cup, they play for the country they call home. Every four years, 32 national teams make it to the men's tournament. For the women, 24 teams qualified in 2019,

Countries from around the world compete in the World Cup.

but the field was expanded to 32 for the 2023 Women's World Cup.

The tournament is played in two stages. The first stage is called group stage. Each group is made up of four teams. Each team plays all the other teams in its group. In a 32-team tournament, the two teams with the best records from each group advance to the next stage.

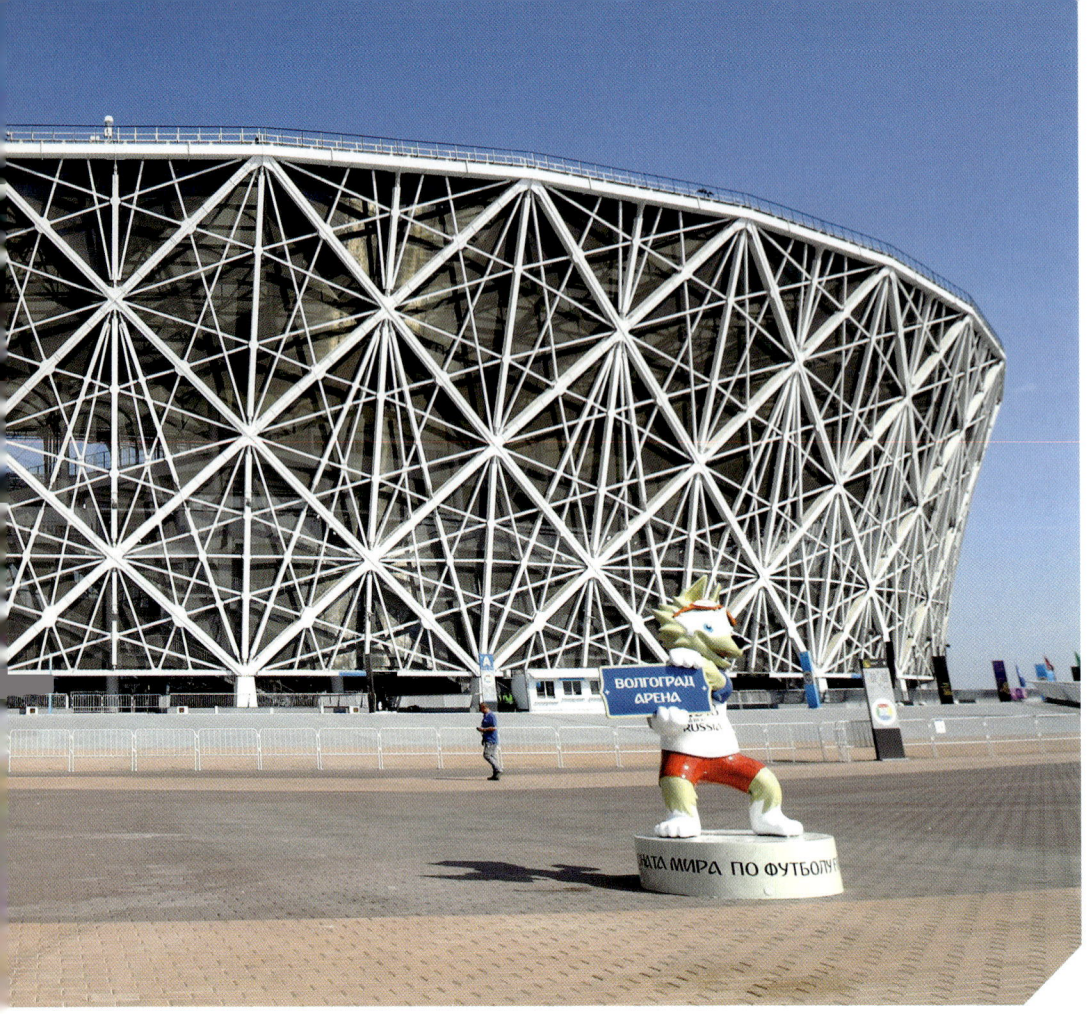

It takes careful planning to build stadiums for the World Cup.

The second stage is a knockout tournament. Once a team loses, it is eliminated. The last two teams standing play in the championship game. The whole tournament lasts more than a month.

Russia hosted the 2018 World Cup. The games were played in 12 stadiums throughout the country.

More than 3 million people saw games played in person. That is only a fraction of the total number of people who watched matches around the world. More than 3 billion people tuned in to watch the games on television over the course of the tournament.

STEM ALL AROUND

Science, technology, engineering, and math (STEM) are a big part of the World Cup. A lot of science about nutrition and movement is used to make training regimens. Keeping players healthy requires athletic trainers and doctors. The official game ball is put through hundreds of scientific tests.

In order for organizers to pull off such a huge event, they need security technology that helps keep fans safe. They also need technology that makes games more accessible. For example, a fan who is visually impaired can use a headset to listen to audio descriptions of what is happening in the game. High-tech equipment is needed to broadcast games to the World Cup's massive television audience.

World Cup organizers also need to use engineering and math. Each new host country has to build or update stadiums. They also need to predict the number of fans who might attend to make sure each event city has enough hotel rooms and food.

Math is used a lot in soccer. It is used to decide which teams advance through the tournament. Referees use math to figure out how much time to add to the clock at the end of a half. From organizers to athletic trainers, the World Cup uses cutting-edge STEM knowledge to create the biggest tournament in the world.

Knowing the STEM concepts in the World Cup can make watching the games even more exciting.

Science explains the motion of the soccer ball.

12

CHAPTER 2

SOCCER SCIENCE

A player sets up for a cross-field pass. He plants one foot. The other foot swings down for a hard kick. It might seem like the foot is the only force that acts on the ball. In reality, many forces are acting on the ball as it travels through the air. Forces act on an object in motion. They can speed up an object, like when a soccer ball is kicked. They can also slow down an object.

One force is gravity. Gravity pulls objects back toward the ground. The strength of gravity depends on an object's mass. The more mass an object has, the stronger gravity pulls objects toward it. Earth's mass is enormous. It pulls the ball toward the ground. A goalie can kick a ball in a high arc. Then gravity tugs the ball back down to the ground.

Another force is drag. Drag is caused by air resistance. As an object moves, air rushes over its surface. This interaction causes the object to slow down. It can even change the way an object moves. Drag can have a big impact on a soccer ball. Each World Cup uses a new ball designed specially for that tournament. Drag has different effects on different ball designs. In 2010 the World Cup ball's design caused a lot of extra drag. Players complained that it affected their passes and shots on goal.

STADIUM SOUNDS

Every World Cup game is jam-packed with fans. The biggest stadium to host a World Cup was Camp Nou in Barcelona, Spain. It hosted matches during the 1982

Fans packed Camp Nou for the opening ceremony.

World Cup. The stadium could fit 120,000 fans. With that many people, the sound can be deafening.

Sound is measured in decibels. A louder sound means more decibels. For example, someone whispering is approximately 30 decibels. Even far away, a jet engine can be more than 100 decibels.

Fans of all ages enjoyed blowing vuvuzelas in the 2010 World Cup.

Really loud sounds can be dangerous. Sound is a wave. Sound waves vibrate a membrane in the ear. If the sound is more than 120 decibels, it can cause that membrane to be injured. That is why it might be a good idea to bring ear protection to a World Cup. In the stands, fans can create sustained sound levels of more than 90 decibels. At the 2010 World Cup in South Africa, fans added to the noise with vuvuzelas. These long plastic trumpets make a loud, high-pitched buzzing sound. Sound scientists estimated that the addition of vuvuzelas raised the crowd noise to 131 decibels at times. It was so loud that some fans reported temporary hearing loss.

Even without a vuvuzela, stadiums are loud. But one sound is the most important. All players need to be able to hear a referee's whistle. So it is usually the loudest sound. A normal whistle might be more than 100 decibels. But a soccer referee's whistle is created with huge crowds in mind. A single blast from the whistle is almost 130 decibels. Even in the loudest stadium, that whistle stands out in a crowd, especially since vuvuzelas have now been banned at the World Cup.

STAYING FIT WITH SLEEP

Soccer is an exhausting game. Players run for a long time. They are also constantly thinking and reacting. Soccer tires the body and the brain. When it comes to the World Cup, the stakes are high. Players have to focus

DECIBELS AND HEARING LOSS

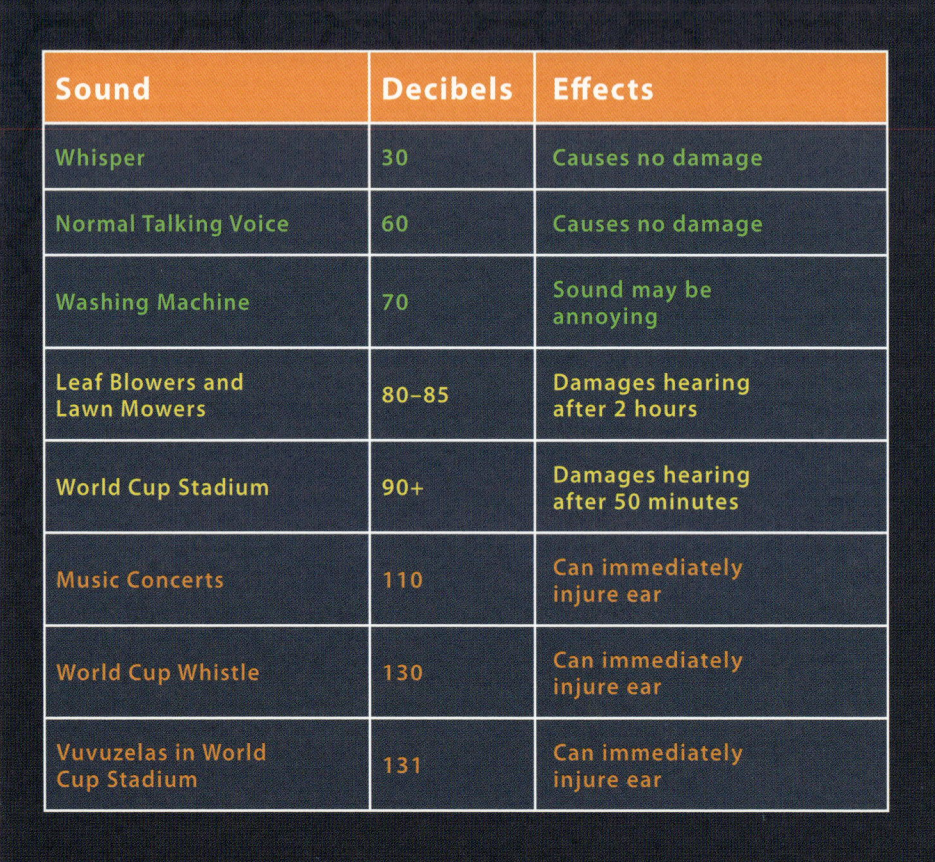

Sound	Decibels	Effects
Whisper	30	Causes no damage
Normal Talking Voice	60	Causes no damage
Washing Machine	70	Sound may be annoying
Leaf Blowers and Lawn Mowers	80–85	Damages hearing after 2 hours
World Cup Stadium	90+	Damages hearing after 50 minutes
Music Concerts	110	Can immediately injure ear
World Cup Whistle	130	Can immediately injure ear
Vuvuzelas in World Cup Stadium	131	Can immediately injure ear

There are lots of loud sounds at the World Cup. The human ear can hear a range of sounds. When things get loud enough, it can cause permanent hearing damage. This infographic shows the decibels of various everyday sounds and World Cup games sounds. Every increase in 10 decibels is equal to a doubling in the intensity of a sound. So a sound that is 40 decibels is twice as powerful as a sound that is 30 decibels. Some of these sounds can lead to hearing problems. By knowing what is too loud, you can take steps to protect your hearing.

on staying healthy. While a player needs to exercise and eat right, getting enough sleep is equally important.

Sleep is a type of recovery. World Cup players use a lot of energy. They use up a lot of hormones, such as adrenaline. Adrenaline boosts blood and oxygen flow in the body. Sleep helps reset the body. When athletes sleep, their bodies are able to rest. Players who do not get enough rest might not be able to play at the top of their game. They might even have a higher risk of injury. Since the World Cup tournament lasts more than a month, players need to have a strict sleep schedule. The goal is to stick to a solid six to eight hours of sleep a night.

CONCUSSION PROTOCOL

Sometimes players get concussions. A concussion is when the brain has been injured. Concussions can be serious. After a head injury, team doctors perform a concussion protocol before a player can return to the game. They check the player's balance. If a player's brain is injured, he or she might not be able to walk straight or stand up. They also ask the player questions to test for confusion.

Cameras are an important part of World Cup security.

CHAPTER 3

GAME TECH

Security is a big deal at the World Cup. The host nation has to ramp up its security in a couple of ways. First, it needs to make sure everyone who comes to the stadium is safe. Then a host country needs to protect its stadiums and fans online. New technology plays an important role in achieving these goals.

One way the World Cup has tried to protect fans is with facial recognition software. Facial recognition software identifies faces. In a crowd of thousands of fans, a camera can pick out a particular face. This can help police track a thief. The authorities can load the software with pictures of known criminals. If the software sees one of the faces, police can move in before something goes wrong. It can also be used to find a lost family member who got separated from a group.

Security also needs to prevent cyberattacks. A cyberattack is when someone tries to hurt people or companies online. One example is phishing. A cyberattacker might send an email with a link to a fake ticket website. Excited fans looking for cheap tickets click on the link. They enter their information into the fake website. The cyber attacker now has all of their personal information. Governments try to protect fans by educating them about the risk of these fake sites.

TECH IN STADIUMS

Technology is also important inside the stadium. At the 2018 World Cup in Russia, half of all purchases

During the 2018 World Cup, Oleg Semyonov ran a call center to help fans with ticket fraud and scams.

were contactless. Contactless payment uses a technology called radio-frequency identification (RFID). RFID is a system that can read a credit card's information without having to touch it. With a contact system, a person has to insert the card into a card reader. Then they have to wait. But contactless payment happens by quickly hovering the card over the reader. People can even load their cards into a smartphone app. Then they

CONTACTLESS PAYMENT

Open the app on phone

Wave the phone over the credit card terminal. This makes a connection using NFC.

User is asked to enter a password or scan fingerprint to confirm payment.

Credit card terminal asks the card company if the card is valid and if there is enough money available. If so, payment is complete.

A chip called the secure element notifies the credit card terminal that the payment was confirmed by user.

Contactless payment is almost like sending a text to the bank. The diagram shows the steps that happen when making a contactless payment. It all happens within seconds. Some of the steps, such as scanning a fingerprint, make the process more secure than other credit card payment methods.

Interpreters help people who are both deaf and blind follow World Cup matches by using a model soccer field.

don't have to take their cards out of their wallets. It's like scanning an item at a grocery store. It is fast and easy, which helps fans get back to the game faster after grabbing a snack.

Technology in the stadiums can also help people who are visually impaired and cannot see the action taking place on the field. Technology can help them keep track of the game. Audio description headphones are available at many World Cup matches. These headphones are tuned into a special commentator. This commentator gives detailed narration of what is happening. The commentator says who has the ball, who

Before a referee can review a play using VAR, a team of officials quickly selects the cameras that most likely caught the best angle on the play.

gets a pass, and all of the other movements of the game. This way a visually impaired fan can be in the stands and cheer right along with the crowd while always knowing what is going on in the game.

VIDEO ASSISTANT REFEREE

A lot of sports have instant replay. Instant replay lets officials review a controversial play. This allows them to make the right call. For the World Cup, instant replay has a special name. It is called video assistant referee (VAR).

VAR uses cameras placed all over the stadium. In soccer one of the most common penalties is offsides.

That happens when there is no defender between an offensive player and the goalie before the ball is kicked to the offensive player. Sometimes a player who scores a goal is called offsides. VAR lets the officials look at the replay to see if it was the right call.

VAR made its first World Cup appearance in 2018. Sometimes it overturned big plays. Two goals were called back. Seven fouls were also called when the referees reviewed the video. FIFA claimed that VAR resulted in accurate calls 99.3 percent of the time. There were just two plays where it was unclear if the referee had made the right call, even after reviewing the video. VAR had a major impact on soccer games and will continue to do so in future World Cups.

CREATING DIGITAL SOCCER PLAYERS

Each year, EA Sports produces a FIFA soccer video game. The game features a World Cup mode. The company produces lifelike models of real players. It also focuses on creating realistic soccer moves. They study signature moves of specific players. In the game, those players are programmed to perform those specific moves.

World Cup stadiums can be expensive to build, and they may not be used much after the event.

28

CHAPTER

4

ENGINEERING THE GAMES

Hosting a World Cup comes with a lot of engineering needs. One of the biggest challenges for a host country is having enough stadiums. A host country might have a professional soccer league. It would then have some stadiums already. However, World Cup stadiums have to be big enough to hold many thousands of people. A host country may need to build some new stadiums for the event.

Building new stadiums can be controversial, though. They are expensive.

When Brazil hosted the World Cup in 2014, it spent $3 billion on stadiums for the tournament. That was more than one-third of the total cost to host the tournament. Another issue is that these stadiums are often only used for the World Cup. Once the tournament is over, countries might not have a use for them. They fall into disrepair.

Qatar is trying to anticipate this problem. It will host the tournament in 2022. At least one of its stadiums will be temporary. The stadium will be built of recycled shipping containers. This building is designed to be taken apart. It could be rebuilt somewhere else later if Qatar needs a new stadium in a different city. It could also be broken up into smaller facilities.

FOOTBALL STADIUMS FOR SOCCER

The United States will cohost the 2026 World Cup with Canada and Mexico. Many people thought the United States would be able to host the games in American football stadiums. However, some of those stadiums aren't wide enough. Soccer fields are 210 to 240 feet (64–73 m) wide. Football fields are usually only around 160 feet (49 m) wide.

Although Qatar is building one stadium that could be moved or broken down, it is also building and expanding on other permanent stadiums.

ARTIFICIAL TURF AT WOMEN'S GAMES

Soccer can be played on either grass or artificial turf. Artificial turf is engineered grass. It is made of synthetic material like nylon. Nylon ropes are woven into yarn. The yarn is woven into a carpet. The carpet is cut into large sections. When artificial turf is on the field, it looks like real grass.

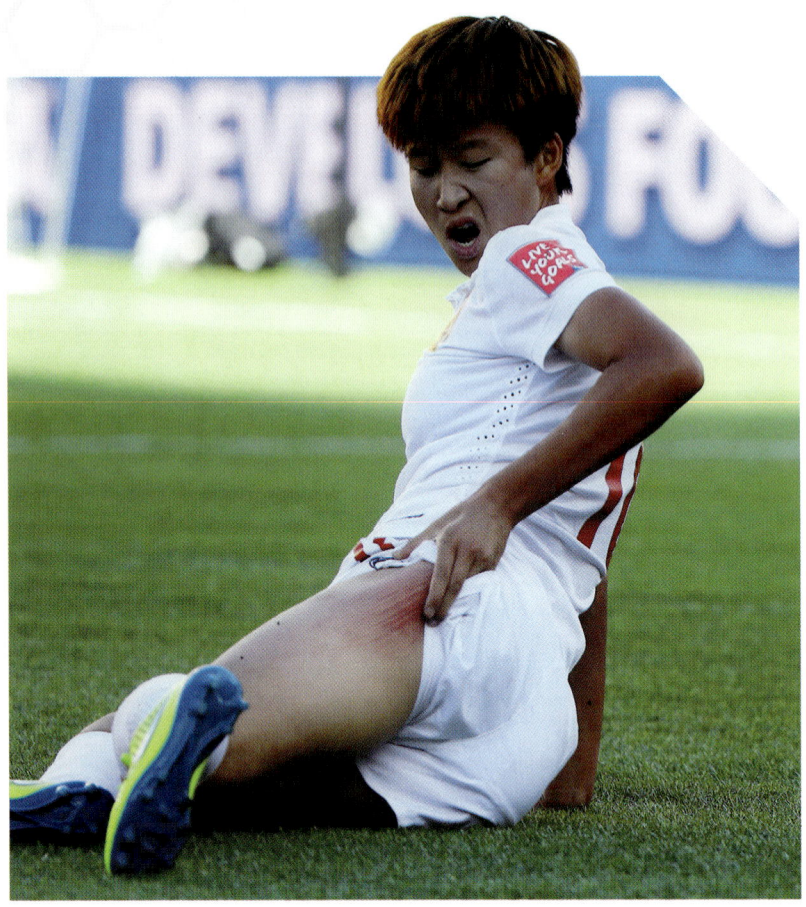

Some players suffered painful turf burn in the 2015 Women's World Cup.

An advantage of turf is that it always plays the same. Real grass might go brown and die. When it's wet, it can be slippery and muddy. With turf there's no worry about bugs eating the field. Every time players step onto a turf field, they know exactly how a ball will roll. Since the field is smoothed out before turf is laid, there are fewer chances of a bumpy surface. Turf also has lower resistance than grass. That means it has less friction. The ball can move faster.

However, many players do not like turf. The 2015 Women's World Cup in Canada was played on turf. Players complained of turf burn. When they slid on the turf, the material caused red and raw patches on their exposed skin. Team doctors also argued that the ground under the turf was too hard and could cause more injuries.

Turf in the Women's World Cup caused controversy. Many argued that the men's tournament would never use turf. Grass is more expensive to maintain. People argued that officials weren't willing to spend the same amount of money for a women's tournament. Even the newest engineered materials might not be the best option for a sport.

TESTING THE GAME BALL

Creating the official World Cup game ball is a feat of engineering. Designers have to pick out the material.

Goalies found the 2010 Jabulani ball unpredictable.

Then they have to design how the ball is put together. They also have to make sure those materials do not interfere with game play. That's where rigorous testing comes into play. Engineers have to run many tests on new designs to make sure they work how they are supposed to.

Testing for balls is done in wind tunnels. A ball is placed in a wind tunnel. Researchers flip a switch, and jets of smoke start flowing around the ball. The jets are lit up by lasers. Researchers can see how the air flows around the ball. They can change the speed of the air, simulating a ball traveling slower or faster.

The 2010 World Cup ball caused players trouble. It had a strange spin to it. When players kicked it, it didn't always go the direction they excepted. Using a wind tunnel, researchers figured out why. One type of shot is a knuckleball. A knuckleball shot spins in a way that causes the ball to zigzag. With traditional soccer balls, this knuckling happens at approximately

NASA engineers tested the 2014 World Cup ball to see how air flowed around it.

30 miles per hour (50 km/h). Professional soccer players kick harder, approximately 50 miles per hour (80 km/h). However, the 2010 ball was designed differently. It was much smoother than a traditional ball. It caused knuckling to happen at 50 miles per hour (80 km/h). That meant goalies had a hard time predicting where the ball might go. In the next years, ball designers were sure to make the ball's surface rougher.

ANATOMY OF THE 2018 WORLD CUP BALL

1970 TELSTAR

2014 BRAZUCA

2018 TELSTAR 18

World Cup balls used to be composed of a number of panels that were stitched together. The 1970 Telstar ball was made to be easily visible on black-and-white television. Today, the ball has been streamlined. The 2014 ball had generally good feedback. The 2018 ball was made with the goal of it moving similarly to the 2014 ball. The 2018 design had 30 percent more seams than the previous 2014 ball, which makes it rougher. That means it would knuckle at a slower speed. So designers made the seams a bit shallower to compensate. This helped give the ball a similar roughness to the 2014 ball.

Goals aren't the only type of points in the World Cup.

CHAPTER **5**

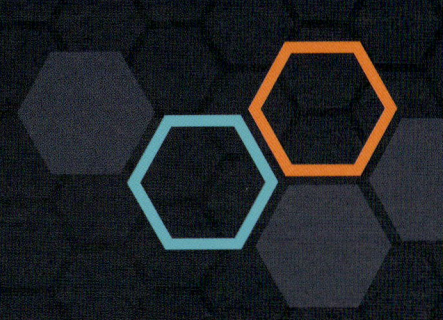

MATH AND NUMBERS

Math is involved in every aspect of the World Cup. The winner of the World Cup is the team with the most points at the end of the last game. However, in the World Cup, points don't only come from scoring goals. There are two types of points that matter. In the first round of play, the numbers are more complicated.

In the group stage, each team plays the other three teams in its group. Teams earn three points for winning a game. If they tie, each will earn one point. They get no points if they lose a game. The two teams with the most points in those three games move on to the next round of play.

Teams might be tied at the end of group play. Officials then look at the goal differential, or how many goals a team scored compared to how many they gave up. One team might have scored 7 goals across its three games and allowed 2 goals. The goal differential is 5. The other team might have scored 7 goals and allowed 3. The goal differential is 4. The team with the goal differential of 5 advances through the tiebreaker. If the goal differentials are the same, officials will break the tie by looking at the total number of goals scored. The team that scored more goals overall will advance. But the World Cup champion is still determined by the winning score in the final game.

CALCULATING STOPPAGE TIME

When it comes to the game clock, soccer differs from sports like basketball and football. First, the time counts

In the 2019 Women's World Cup, the United States beat Thailand 13–0 in the group stage. That gave the United States a big advantage in goal differential.

up, not down. In a basketball game, the clock starts at 12 minutes and counts down to zero. In soccer the clock starts at zero and runs up to 90 minutes, with a break for halftime at 45 minutes. And in soccer, the clock never stops. Other sports have time-outs, or the clock stops when the ball goes out of bounds. But with soccer, once the clock starts, it just keeps going. Because of this, soccer has a special rule called stoppage time.

The time it takes to prepare for a free kick is included in stoppage time.

Stoppage time is added on to the end of each half. A referee keeps track of how long play stops in a game. Play might stop because a player was hurt. It might also stop because of a penalty or when players celebrate after a goal. It also stops when referees have to review a play with VAR. At the end of the half, the referee adds all those stops together. Then the referee adds that much time on to the end of the half. Stoppage time is usually between one and six minutes.

However, the math is pretty imprecise. For the 2018 World Cup, journalists carefully calculated how long play stopped in each game. Then they compared their numbers to the stoppage time that referees added. They found that almost all games didn't have enough time added to them. On average, 7 minutes were added to the game. But the journalists found that that average total time that play stopped was 14 minutes.

The journalists also did the math to figure out which activities take up the most stoppage time. They found that the biggest chunk of time was free kicks. Free kicks accounted for almost 10 percent of all stoppage time. On average, 10 minutes per game are spent setting up free kicks. The activity that took the least amount of stoppage time was for arguments. That only took up

STOPPAGE TIME PERCENTAGES

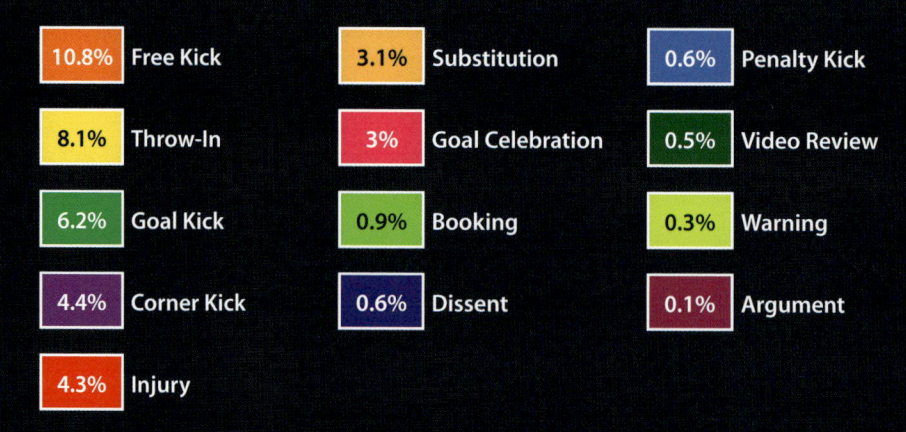

Regular Game Play 57.1%

10.8% Free Kick	3.1% Substitution	0.6% Penalty Kick
8.1% Throw-In	3% Goal Celebration	0.5% Video Review
6.2% Goal Kick	0.9% Booking	0.3% Warning
4.4% Corner Kick	0.6% Dissent	0.1% Argument
4.3% Injury		

Game play stops for a lot of reasons. Luckily, most of the time it stops for things like throwing the ball in or for penalty kicks. But every once in a while, the game stops because a player gets a yellow or red card, meaning the player has committed a foul. It can also stop because a player is arguing with the ref.

approximately 0.1 percent of all stoppage time. So if an argument did happen, it didn't last very long.

UNDERSTANDING THE WORLD CUP

STEM will continue to play a big part in the World Cup. Science will help fans understand how to protect their ears. Technology helps security keep fans safe. Engineering allows people to make safer and more sustainable stadiums. And math will continue to create exciting tournaments. With all this STEM excitement, the World Cup is sure to remain the biggest sporting event in the world.

A LUCKY OCTOPUS

Some numbers in the World Cup are silly. For example, in 2010 people fell in love with Paul the octopus. Paul was presented with two boxes of food. The food was the same in each box. But the boxes were decorated with different team flags. Whichever box Paul ate from first, people said that was his prediction for the winner of the match. Paul correctly picked all seven of Germany's wins and losses. He also correctly picked the ultimate winner, Spain. The chance of making those correct picks was 1 in 256.

GLOSSARY

concussion
A brain injury caused by impact.

disrepair
Falling apart; needing repair.

friction
Resistance that happens when one object rubs against another.

mass
A measure of how much matter is in an object.

membrane
A thin layer of tissue or muscle.

plants
Places down firmly.

resistance
A force pushing back against an object.

simulating
Recreating a real-world situation.

synthetic
Fake, made by humans.

visually impaired
Having poor sight or being blind.

MORE INFORMATION

BOOKS

Carothers, Thomas. *Women's World Cup Heroes*. Minneapolis, MN: Abdo Publishing, 2019.

Marquardt, Meg. *STEM in Soccer*. Minneapolis, MN: Abdo Publishing, 2018.

Moussavi, Sam. *World Cup Heroes*. Minneapolis, MN: Abdo Publishing, 2019.

ONLINE RESOURCES

Booklinks
NONFICTION NETWORK
FREE! ONLINE NONFICTION RESOURCES

To learn more about STEM in the World Cup, visit **abdobooklinks.com** or scan this QR code. These links are routinely monitored and updated to provide the most current information available.

Camp Nou, 14
concussions, 19
contactless payment, 23–25
cyberattacks, 22

decibels, 15–17, 18
drag, 14

gravity, 13–14
group stage, 7, 39–40

knockout tournament, 8

Paul the octopus, 45
points, 39–40

Qatar, 30

Russia, 8, 22

video assistant referee (VAR), 26–27, 43

wind tunnel, 35
World Cup
 2010, 14, 16, 35–36, 45
 2014, 30, 37
 2018, 8, 22, 27, 37, 43
 2026, 30

ABOUT THE AUTHOR

Meg Marquardt started her career as a scientist but decided she liked writing about science even more. She enjoys researching physics, geology, and climate science. She lives in Madison, Wisconsin, with her two scientist cats, Lagrange and Doppler.